Swimming in a Thunderstorm

by kelly giles

featuring cover art by Mark Moya

Limited first edition

First published June, 2011

www.kgstoryteller.com

www.booksbyprescription.com

Copyright 2011 Kelly Giles

All rights reserved.

ISBN 978-0-578-08711-5

"There is no order in the world around us....
Let others bring order to chaos.
I will bring chaos to order"
-Kurt Vonnegut, <u>Breakfast of Champions</u>

"People wish to be settled. It is only as far as they are unsettled that there is any hope for them."
Emerson, Ralph Waldo

"Listen to presences inside poems, Let them take you where they will. Follow those private hints, And never leave the premises."
   - Rumi (The Tent)

"WE DON'T READ AND WRITE POETRY BECAUSE IT'S CUTE. WE READ AND WRITE POETRY BECAUSE WE ARE MEMBERS OF THE HUMAN RACE. AND THE HUMAN RACE IS FILLED WITH PASSION. AND MEDICINE, LAW, BUSINESS, ENGINEERING, THESE ARE NOBLE PURSUITS AND NECESSARY TO SUSTAIN LIFE. BUT POETRY, BEAUTY, ROMANCE, LOVE, THESE ARE WHAT WE STAY ALIVE FOR." ~DEAD POET'S SOCIETY~

"What is a poet? An unhappy man who in his heart harbors a deep anguish, but whose lips are so fashioned that the moans and cries which pass over them are transformed into ravishing music." –Kierkegaard

"…it is the attempt at 'everyone' that matters regardless of the cost; to live as an aesthete is to declare in effect that the versatility is worth the melancholy." – Louis Mackey, "Kierkegaard: A kind of Poet"

"One joy scatters a hundred griefs." – Chinese proverb

Gracious Failures

Desiring darkness
    Presence punishes
        Shameful sacrifice
Fearing forgiveness
    Painful peace
        Jarring joy
Subversive spirit
    Gracious guilt
        Abandoned adoptee
Freeing failures
    Condemning compassion
        Denying despair
Humbling humanity
    Alienated adoptee
        Baptized brokenness
    Craving compassion
Embracing enemies
    Forgiving friends
        Desiring deliverance

Seven months

Lost complacency
        Terrifyingly helpless

Fears otherness
        Adoptive compassion

Grateful outsider
        Fears belonging

Abandonment humiliates
        Indifference infuriates

Lies linger
        Attacks anger

Brokenness blesses
        Cowardice challenges

Dependence damages
        Dependence dignifies

Enemies energize
        Forgiveness frees

birthday poem
(inspired by rumi, "having nothing")
water womb/child's heart

starving spring

        stillness pours

ultimate chaos

        thirst captures

needs breast

        mother's pain

burning cries

        distressed infant

tender pain

        floating womb

water words

        lips answer

build openings

        marvelous need

hands answer

        question pain

difficult cure

        secret provisions

needing nothing

        child's language

bears bruises

        heals hearts

    Divinely despairing

Hidden hatred

    Kills humanity

Blinds spirit

    Denies stress

Vengefully certain

    Hatefully complacent

Pretentiously self-satisfied

    Fearfully respectable

Intolerantly scapegoats

    Benignly doubtful

Creatively confused

    Divinely despairing

Productively depressed

    Accepts suffering

Acknowledges weakness

    Wisely respectful

Experiences empathy

Everything is upside down

    For the God I believe in is

        A terrified detainee

            Being tortured to death

                By a terrified soldier

            Because we were told

        To take the gloves off

        A native American

            Drinking himself to death

        An Indian immigrant

            Being shot & killed

                For wearing a turban

        Too soon after 9/11

        A gay man

            Being brutally beaten to death

        A raw recruit

            Left paralyzed for life

                And speaking out

            Against the madness of war

An abortionist

    Suffering severe facial injuries

        When her clinic is firebombed

A grey & white stray cat

    Being hit by a car

        & being cared for by my neighbor & i

    Who the animal hospital said

        They could try to save

            For 75 dollars

    But when we called animal control

        They said our referral had died

            Thus saving the city 75 dollars

A stop-lossed soldier

    Killing himself

        Rather than returning to the hell

    He thought he'd finally been freed from

A prostitute

    Being viciously raped

        By a moralistic vigilante

A journalist

    At the Palestine hotel

        Being killed

    For trying to tell the truth

        About the war

A Japanese father

    Being detained at Manzanar

        Because he looked

    Like an enemy combatant

An undocumented trans-gendered immigrant

    Dying in terminal island (how aptly named)!

        Detention center

    Because we won't let him have

        His HIV med's

But when everything is right side up

    The God I believe in will be

        A homeless street kid

            Welcoming an army of orphans

                Into a family of gangbangers

            In search of the ultimate rave

    & when we finally find

The rave to end all raves

    The music will rip our hearts out

        & we'll never again

    Be able to forget

How loved we've always been

      Healing hunger

Obsessively open

      Compulsively compassionate

Rituals reassure

      Confusingly controlling

Possessively panic-stricken

      Resists regression

Dreads dependence

      Vilifies vulnerability

Narcissistically nurturing

      Authority alienates

Self-destructively seductive

      Healing hunger

Purposeful pain

      Welcomes wounding

Trust terrifies

      Innocence irritates

Peacefully playful

      Sacrificially sexual

Accepts affirmation

Beneath the Mask

Unworthy identity
    Angrily alone
Abandons rescuers
    Tearfully independent
Ungratefully belonging
    Anxiously bewildered
Disrespectfully questioning
    Secretively hurting
Relationally rebellious
    Closeness complicates
Love liberates

Beneath the mask3 (chapter 3)

Secret shame
    Grieving guilt
Blindly blaming
    Angrily abandoning
Anxiously aloof
    Hostilely honest
Defensively disloyal
    Painfully persevering
Obstinately open
    Edgily empathetic
Tentatively trusting

Beneath the Mask4a (chapter 4a)

AKA: Primally protected

Angrily anxious

    Lost love

Narcissistically nurturing

    Purposeful pain

Happiness hurts

    Fearfully furious

Traumatically trusting

    Darkly depressed

Sensitively struggling

    Primally protected

Beneath the mask4b

(aka: guardedly grieving)

Painfully patient

    Permanently persevering

Liberating loss

    Securely separated

Anxiously affirming

    Respectfully rejecting

Ambiguously attached

    Guardedly grieving

Disconnectedly distancing

    Traumatically trusting

Sorrowfully supportive

    Hidden hunger

Fearfully fragile

    Loyalty liberates

Humor heals

Beneath the Mask5

Silent safety

    Anxiously affirming

Furiously frozen

    Secret sadness

Hopelessly honest

    Supportively separating

Accepts angst

    Daringly depressive

Adventurously apprehensive

    Lost loyalty

Intimately isolated

    Healing harshness

Impulsively insightful

    Obstinately open

Welcomes wounded

    Saves self

Beneath the Mask 6

Cries confusion
> Hidden hopelessness

Loss liberates
> Intimacy intimidates

Rituals reassure
> Safe secrecy

Suicidal stoicism
> Traumatically trusting

Understanding unifies
> Vanity vilifies

Anxiously angry
> Deceptively disruptive

Disturbingly disengaged
> Demandingly distant

Courageous closure
> Overwhelmingly open

Sadly sabotaging
> Heartbreakingly hopeful

Angrily alone
> Derision depresses

Faces fears
> Acceptance absolves

Beneath the Mask 7

Resilient resistance
      Defiantly distrustful
Fears fragmentation
      Deprivation detaches
Anger attaches
      Abandons affection
Helplessness hurts
      Sensitively suffering
Guardedly grieving
      Anxiously aggressive
Unbearably understanding
      Mourning misfortune
Change confuses
      Darkly despairing
Healing helplessness
      Terrifyingly trusting
Represses revulsion
      Closure comforts
Resists rescue
      Sorrowfully suspicious
Overwhelmingly open
      Tenderly trusting

　　　　　Secret sadness

Angry avoidance

　　　Child-like confusion

Secret sadness

　　　Ambivalently appreciative

Rejects relationships

　　　Safely suspicious

Distrusts dependence

　　　Derisively defensive

Honestly helpless

　　　Welcomes warmth

        Angrily wounded

Angrily wounded
        Darkly lost
Addictively rejecting
        Rebelliously vulnerable
Wildly distant
        Hopelessly empty
Disconnectedly unavailable
        Hides abandonment
Fears failure
        Confronts confusion
Verbalizes vulnerability
        Tentatively trusts

        Exposed despair

Exposed despair

    Drowning fears

Impostor clings

    Forgotten failure

Spirit thrives

    Survives darkness

Lost struggles

    Sorrows endure

Despair darkens

    Clouded tunnel

Joy's light

    Hope's harness

Pleadingly praising

　　　　　　Welcoming weakness

Welcoming weakness

　　　　Passionately present

Freely frightened

　　　　Understandably unbearable

Dangerously distressed

　　　　Calmly coherent

Empathetically exploring

　　　　Wrenchingly withdrawing

Difficulties dissociate

　　　　Intentionally integrates

Stubbornly self-sufficient

　　　　Healingly helpless

Understanding uplifts

　　　　Love liberates

Trust transforms

        Stricken shepherd

Precious doubt

      Caring strength

Fighting love

      Fears demise

Dark despair

      Wounded weeping

Buried anger

      Submerged sorrow

Stricken shepherd

      Helpless heart

Craves consolation

      Abandonment aches

Questions calling

      Harbors hope

Curses cruelty

      Seeks salvation

Fears fragmentation

      Wants wholeness

Grasps grace

Soul Confusion

confusion

Longing survives

Secret darkness

Heart's night

Realistic rope

Hell's doorstep

Losing lifelines

Reconsiders calling

Confirms desperation

Desires inspiration

Fears isolation

Considers adaptation

Lacks information

Craves confirmation

Needs transformation

Wilderness identity

Tragic self-reliance

Awakened vulnerability

Deeply controlling

Darkly punishing

Angrily absent

Painfully anxious

Aching rejection

Tears comfort

Despairingly powerless

Wilderness identity

Autonomous heart

Craves connection

Fears submission

Seeks surrender

Openly outcast

Questions value

Fights intimacy

Wearily disconnected

Freedom frightens

Wants wisdom

Father's forgiveness

Heart's home

    Fearfully courageous

Unbearable hell
    Overwhelming desperation
Chaotic hope
    Empty horizon
Storms paralyze
    Painful betrayal
Fearfully courageous
    Unsustainably angry
Hopelessly sinking
    Unrecognizably powerless
Traumatically alone
    Empathy connects
Recognition restores

    Child's heart

Abandonment's despair
    Denial's emptiness
Desires escape
    Dignity's delight
Disconnectedly driven
    Meaning affirms
Honors purpose
    Fears poverty
Aloneness shames
    Losing authority
Accusations entomb
    Acceptance ennobles
Divinely loved
    Confusingly cursed
Passivity paralyzes
    Empathy energizes
Child's heart
    Needs nurturing

    Lifeblood lingers

Damaged soul

    Desperately tortured

Fears drowning

    Hides despair

Exposes hopelessness

    Sinking corpse

Swallows waves

    Lifeblood lingers

Curse chokes

    Blessing breathes

Love's lifeline

    Bandages brokenness

Soothes soul

Navigating nightmares

Nightmarish calling

    Navigating failures

Delegating ruination

    Destructive blame

Painfully disastrous

    Passionately rescuing

Dangerously idealistic

    Poisonous injustice

Forever fighting

    Wants wisdom

Finds forgiveness

Containing chaos

Heroic death
    Villainous life
Placates persecutors
    Abandons victims
Helpless rescuer
    Ordinary slaughter
Overwhelms sheep
    Traumatic shelter
Survives failures
    Shell-shocked denial
Delusional loser
    Fears cling
Misses meaning
    Bottomless dungeon
Buries sorrow
    Dizzying depths
Breaks bondage
    Escapes emptiness
Contains chaos

       Battling Blindness

Chaotic achiever
       Desperate fighter
Contained desire
       Deepest nightmare
Navigated depths
       Denies stress
Despair tears
       Physical collapse
Acknowledges unworthiness
       Irrationally escapes
Rationally admits
       Seeks sanity
Finds fragility
       Battles blindness
Desires deliverance
       Craves clarity
Injustice infuriates
       Loss liberates
Acceptance alleviates
       Empathy elevates

Primal Scream

Primal cowardice
      Screams forgiveness
Covers ashes
      Deceit crawls
Shame survives
      Acknowledges terror
Confesses cowardice
      Painful prayer
Good guilt
      Hides hurt
Protects clients
      Desperately delivers
Legalistic slaughter
      Stubbornly secretive
Tentatively trusting
      Truth terrifies
Love lingers
      Achingly accepted

Denial Dissolves

Crushed confidence
    Nightmarish depths
Obsessively overwhelming
    Traumatically trusting
Tragically torn
    Freely escaping
Denial dissolves
    Brutally broken
Edge energizes
    Grace galvanizes
Savagely sacrificed
    Anger annihilates
Sorrow soothes
    Lifeline lingers

Ruined rescuer

Completely vulnerable

    Discontentment drives

Senselessly suffering

    Emptiness engulfs

Despair destroys

    Fear fragments

Wounded writer

    Damaged deliverer

Ruined rescuer

    Stripped self-worth

Hobbled healer

    Accused advocate

Imprisoned idealist

    Bankrupt benefactor

Welcomes wound

    Acknowledges anguish

Desires deliverance

    Trust terrifies

Brokenness beautifies

Craving compassion

Despair terrifies

    Darkest breaking-point

Soul's pain

    Dying hope

Folly frightens

    Questions everything

Hides hopelessness

    Craves compassion

Acknowledges anger

    Suppresses sadness

Misses mercy

    Loses lifeline

Slowly sinking

    Numbs neediness

Peace pursues

    Simplicity soothes

Nowhere boy
(inspired by film of the same name, about john lennon, who was also adopted)

Lost boy

    Fears love

Hopes died

    Finds futility

Senseless slaughter

    Destroys dignity

Ruins reputation

    Self-destructive shame

Fatherless failure

    Abandoned advocate

Broken barrister

    Crushed child

Despondent deliverer

    Stricken shepherd

Weeps inconsolably

    Surrenders unconditionally

Embraces emptiness

    Melts mercifully

      Painfully persevering

Shaken son

      Surgery scares

Financial failure

      Nameless nightmare

Shame survives

      Painfully persevering

Disowned defender

      Trust terrifies

Traumatic transition

      Empathy endures

Seeks safety

      Finds fragmentation

Diligently disorganized

      Chaotically compassionate

Naively noble

      Innocently inspired

Desperately driven

      Compassionately compelled

Unconditionally upheld

    Brilliantly broken

Monumentally torn
    Voices failure
Chaotic struggle
    Mindlessly abandoned
Suffering child
    Senselessly accursed
Forsaken fighter
    Deserted deliverer
Brilliantly broken
    Crushed calling
Agonizing advocate
    Wanders wreckage
Embraces emptiness
    Salvages simplicity

        Imagining illumination

Openly overwhelmed

        Freely frozen

Cursed child

        Passionately panic-stricken

Desires dissociation

        Unreservedly unreal

Nervously numb

        Angrily avoidant

Disconnectedly damaged

        Imagines illumination

Dreams delightedly

        Seeks shelter

Fights fears

        Wants wholeness

Brutally broken

        Beautifully bandaged

      Silent soul

Silent soul

      Deceitfully judged

Praise saves

      Hatred shames

Dishonorably persecuted

      Lying accusers

Afflicted servant

      Lovingkindness lifts

Blesses needy

      Curses greedy

Wickedly wounded

      Desperately despondent

Frighteningly fragile

      Seeks solace

Demands deliverance

      Challenges chaos

Pursues peace

      Welcomes wonder

       Blessedly distressed

Loosed light

    Dark bonds

Upright servant

    Fearful liars

Graciously afflicted

    Compassionately stumbling

Righteous tears

    Heart dies

Eyes enemies

    Bountifully poor

Mindfully sorrowful

    Blessedly distressed

Soul's terrors

    Rescues needy

Longing lifts

    Imagination ignites

Jumpstarts heart

    Necessary growth

Dispiriting past

    Catastrophic future

Suffocating permanence

    Liberating timelessness

Blessedly affirming

    Accepting potential

Securely gifted

    Flexibly growing

Necessarily haunted

    Terrifying present

Defining nightmares

    Urgently responsible

Faithfully surrendering

    Compassionately influencing

Embracing injustice

    Imagining justice

Openly present

    Depression's deliverance

Everlasting distress

    Lovingkindness answers

Good fear

    Violent prosperity

Falling saves

    Thanks helps

Righteous strength

    Salvation song

Discipline's gate

    Death's door

Severe season

    Oppression opens

Depression delivers

    Simplicity sanctifies

       Calming shadows

Overwhelming nightmare

       Bleak survival

Patient dependence

       Calming shadows

Courageous death

       Desperately insightful

Fears initiative

       Unfulfilled potential

Bankrupt shelter

       Shattered self-worth

Understands powerlessness

       Pleadingly praises

Surrender saves

      Torn open

Fragile ship

      Vulnerable haven

Torn dependence

      Relentless mercy

Fosters hope

      Adoptive mourning

Frozen feelings

      Understood cruelty

Torn open

      Primal awareness

Compassionate wounding

      Desperately independent

Fears dependence

      Stubbornly strong

Denies vulnerability

      Terrifyingly tough

Fears fragility

      Crushed cocoon

Broken butterfly

       A paradox

Embedded betrayal

       Resists trust

Embraces vulnerability

       Confusingly futile

Embraces aloneness

       Losing hope

Frozen future

       Painful past

Nightmarish present

       Resistance embeds

Embracing loosens

Sorrowful Song

Hopelessly heartbroken
    Self-doubt strangles

Angrily dependent
    Hostilely vulnerable

Thankfulness suffers
    Imagines provision

Craves alternatives
    Darkly struggling

Seeks safety
    Distressingly distrustful

Playful father
    Encourages imagination

Visionaries fascinate
    Welcomes wonder

Sings sorrowfully
    Embraces utterly

       Courageously tormented

Courageously tormented
       Threatens safety

Attacks security
       Cruelly crushed

Fears fragility
       Desires deliverance

Emptiness envelops
       Achingly alone

Deception devastates
       Business brutalizes

Compassion crawls
       Hope hides

Suffering surrounds
       Patience prays

Gentleness guides
       Brokenness bends

Thankfulness transcends

        Embracing alienation

Anger's darkness

        Suffering's depths

Light endures

        Thankfulness heals

Enemies surround

        Hope hurts

Forgiving future

        Embraces enemies

Isolation alienates

        Confusion cripples

Brokenness opens

        Humility heals

Shame buries

        Despair darkens

Acceptance awakens

        Peace permeates

        Injustice aches

Lost assurance

        Helplessly driven

Wearily paralyzed

        Powerlessly miserable

Fallen failure

        Fighting despair

Fleeing collapse

        Injustice aches

Binds broken-hearted

        Accepts affliction

Forgives failures

        Slowly surrenders

Tentatively trusts

        Mercy melts

Redemptive ruination

Wintry wilderness

Shatters promises

Water sustains

Fights despair

Darkness swallows

Desert surrounds

Light lifts

Imagines innocence

Sorrow suffocates

Senseless suffering

Mercifully meaningful

Redemptive ruination

Tenaciously Trusting

Heart's despair
      Forgiven faithlessness

Openness threatens
      Buries help

Weakness crushes
      Fights support

Assertiveness uplifts
      Heart struggles

Shares confusion
      Loses hope

Finds fragility
      Recaptures relevance

Seeks simplicity
      Trusts tenaciously

Brutalized Heart

Brutalized heart

    Craves compassion

Receives rejection

    Contributions questioned

Needs negated

    Openness blockaded

Welcome withdrawn

    Isolation increases

Dialogue decreases

    Sorrow submerges

Heart hides

        Calming chaos

Addictive emptiness

        Chaotic desperation

Supportive structure

        Motivation elevates

Suffering submerges

        Submission sustains

Compassion compensates

        Mercy melts

Love lifts

        Forgiveness fills

Calms chaos

Sacrificial freedom

Selfish slavery

    Sacrificial freedom

Broken trust

    Bitterly despairing

Wearily pleading

    Openly broken

Angelically obedient

    Humbly needy

Surrendered servant

    Forgiven weakness

Achingly submissive

    Unconditionally embraced

        Creative Chaos

Oppressive order
        Calming chaos
Hollow stability
        Credibility crisis
Barbaric brutality
        Petrified politicians
Massive military
        Empties economy
Creative chaos
        Overturns order

Calming chaos 2

Ferociously straying
  Wildly trusting
Passionately nesting
  Openly tangled
Fearfully unveiled
  Surrender saves
Dependence restores
  Order terrifies
Chaos calms
  Fears structure
Welcomes wildness
  Supports transgressors
Dangerously acquitted
  Strips presumptions
Navigates hiddenness
  Overturns order
Grasps grace

      Soul's control

Betrayed shepherd

      Internally vocal

Externally voiceless

      Injustice aches

Heavenly struggle

      Hellish stability

Soul's control

      Deceptively calm

Destructively isolated

      Externally loved

Internally dead

      Dangerously heroic

Heroically bankrupt

      Externally weak

Internally strong

      Eternally embraced

    Bankrupt heart

Dangerously bitter

    Slowly softening

Bankrupt heart

    Tentatively toughening

Stricken shepherd

    Questions calling

Hardened hearts

    Increase isolation

Desperately drowning

    Openly broken

Screams silently

    Listens longingly

Solitude soothes

Navigating Nastiness

Tearful toughness
    Bloodied fighter

Holy sufferer
    Painfully grateful

Damaged dreamer
    Vilified visionary

Fears closeness
    Desires distance

Shuns security
    Openly overwhelmed

Brutally broken
    Painfully paralyzed

Traumatically terrified
    Navigates nastiness

Appreciates angels
    Tearfully trusting

Wounded heart

Prideful enmity

    Peaceful humility

Chaotic stillness

    Adventurously structured

Sorrowfully comforting

    Joyfully accepting

Fears security

    Welcomes surprises

Dying soul

    Wounded heart

Wandering warrior

    Despairing deliverer

Imagines trusting

    Openly sacrificing

Adventurously accepting

    Securely surfing

Creatively belonging

    Ecstatically embraced

        Ferociously vulnerable

Despair's darkness

    Simplicity's light

Wild woundedness

    Celebrates beauty

Shadows surround

    Dawn's breaking

Fears vulnerability

    Ferociously independent

Troubling tensions

    Open wounds

Suffering swallows

    Joy follows

Longing lingers

    Peace protects

Dawn's embrace

Solitary dawn

    Breaks silence

Faith darkens

    Friends brighten

Prayerfully providing

    Lovingly sustaining

Cruelly wounded

    Despairingly vulnerable

Brokenness buries

    Darkly fragile

Agonizingly abandoned

    Oppressively outcast

Silently suffering

    Miserably marginalized

Intimacy intimidates

    Reconciliation revives

Ecstatically embraced

        Broken healer

Hardships liberate

        Angelic suffering

Dark grace

        Freedom's forgetfulness

Painfully merciful

        Fearfully courageous

Powerfully frail

        Brokenly healed

Sorrowfully happy

        Downwardly mobile

Creatively chaotic

        Openly needy

Welcomes wounds

        Grasps grace

Sheltering Shadows

Leaving home

    Presence sustains

Fear remains

    Violently violated

Hatefully humiliated

    Desperately destroyed

Reputation ruined

    Prayerfully protected

Angelically assisted

    Deafening absurdity

Obediently listening

    Accepts shadows

Shadows shelter

        Cradled orphan

Orphaned pilgrim
        Accepts abandonment
Selflessly present
        Washed-up warrior
Broke barrister
        Withdrawn validation
Terrified heart
        Overfed head
Empty intelligence
        Wants wisdom
Elusive oasis
        Darkest desert
Wanders deeper
        Feels forsaken
Breaks open
        Compassion cradles

Thunderstorm swimmer

Thunderstorm swimmer
    Peaceful provocateur

Chaotically ordered
    Rigidly flexible

Uniquely universal
    Beautifully burdened

Darkly trusting
    Wearily worthwhile

Openly broken
    Humbly honored

Unconditionally upheld
    Silent swimmer

Floats freely

Cradled orphan2

Selfless orphan
    Abandoned savior

Stubbornly solitary
    Beautifully broken

Weakened warrior
    Humbly heroic

Restlessly present
    Deafeningly silent

Overwhelmingly open
    Lonely listener

Craves community
    Tensely trusting

Persistently prayerful
    Welcomes wonder

Compassion cradles

Provocatively powerless

Loathing liberates

    Iciness invigorates

Gratifyingly gifted

    Destructively free

Creatively chained

    Bleakness burns

Awareness struggles

    Damaged pleasures

Fullness fragments

    Scarcity simplifies

Craves control

    Dangerously empty

Writing threatens

    Services sanctifies

Illusory redemption

    Gracefully helpless

Provocatively powerless

    Neediness navigates

Welcomes wounded

    Struggle sanctifies

        Destructively creative

Power kills
    Weakness creates
Comforts afflicted
    Afflicts comfortable
Befriends enemies
    Hatred's love
Despairing hope
    Faithful doubter
Evil's good
    Redemptive sin
Destructively creative
    Prayerfully persecuted
Irrationally attacked
    Addictively avoiding
Obediently suffering
    Criminal church
Criminal Christ?
    Dependence delivers
Father's forgiveness

Glimpsing Stars

Fear deceives

    Destroys trust

Truth deepens

    Passionately protects

Abandons escapades

    Endless deceptions

Massages truth

    Power strips

Glimpses stars

    Unconditionally precious

Love's eyes

    Escapades bankrupt

Fear strips

    Secrets strangle

Lies linger

    Glimpses grace

Love liberates

Desperation

Abandoned orphan
      Selfless savior

Craving control
      Radically trusting

Sacrifices livelihood
      Reputation shattered

Stupidly vulnerable
      Tenderly blind-sided

Darkly despairing
      Bitterly broken

Desperately drowning
      Desperately dreaming

Desperately delivered

        Embracing fragility

Terrifyingly weary

    Nightmarishly burnt-out

Broke barrister

    Miraculously surviving

Traumatically trusting

    Overwhelming possibilities

Welcomes weakness

    Faces fragility

Accepts embrace

       Compassionately despairing

Truly despairing

    Rebellious rescuer

Drowning love

    Grace's darkness

Light's narrowness

    Sacrificial depths

Unconditionally crashing

    Questions calling

Faith's hell

    Traumatizing trials

Achingly abandoned

    Openly broken

Compassionately cradled

       Painfully present

Passively present
       Actively absent
Trusting tenaciously
       Balancing blindly
Scarred soul
       Battling bravely
Spiritually struggling
       Forsaken front-liner
Defeated distance-runner
       Darkness debilitates
Infection infuriates
       Insecurity isolates
Acknowledges ache
       Painfully present
Embraces emptiness
       Welcomes wholeness

        Shaken soul

Trust strips

        Initiates miracles

Illusory guidance

        Divine dependence

Ruined reputation

        Lost livelihood

Fragile friends

        Infection incapacitates

Restoration rejuvenates

        Peace proliferates

Shaken soul

        Forgiveness floods

Healing humbles

        Love liberates

Trust shelters

Defiantly creative

Broken healer

    Brutally wounded

Recklessly bloodied

    Stubbornly tragic

Dreamily responsible

    Fearfully torn

Pridefully denying

    Humbly acknowledging

Abandonment aches

    Adoptively embraced

Brilliantly playful

    Darkly crashing

Embraces imagination

    Defies destroyers

Creativity caresses

www.ingramcontent.com/pod-product-compliance
Lightning Source LLC
Chambersburg PA
CBHW031211090426
42736CB00009B/877